Charlie's Adventures
THE CLOUD KINGDOM

written by Augustine Charles

AUSTIN'S WONDERLAND

Dedication

For my brother Nicholas,
whose magic inspires me to keep
my head in the clouds.

Charlie and the Cloud Kingdom teaches cloud science in a fun and imaginative way. Use the guide below to identify clouds and their correct pronunciation to help guide you when reading the story.
Have fun on your adventure!

Cumulus
[kyoo-myuh-luhs]

Cirrus
[sir-uhs]

Stratus
[strey-tuhs, strat-uhs]

Nimbostratus
[nim-boh-strey-tuhs, -strat-uhs]

Stratocumulus
[strey-toh-kyoo-myuh-luhs, strat-oh-]

Altocumulus
[al-toh-kyoo-myuh-luhs]

Cumulonimbus
[kyoo-myuh-loh-nim-buhs]

Cirrostratus
[sir-oh-strey-tuhs, -strat-uhs]

Arcus
[ahr-kuhs]

Asperitas
[as-pe-ri-tas]

Charlie and his dog Pan spent the afternoon staring up at the sky and pointing out the different shapes the clouds made. Pan was really excited about a biscuit-shaped cloud. He imagined how delicious it would be if he could just have one bite.

Charlie had learned the names for the different
types of clouds in his science class at school. He saw cumulus
clouds, cirrus clouds, and cirrostratus clouds floating above.
"One day, I'll touch them," Charlie said to Pan as they drifted
off to sleep.

When Charlie opened his eyes he was met with a big surprise. He was surrounded by clouds that looked like people gathered near a tall castle.

One of the cloud people guided him through the castle's doors.

Standing before him was King Cirrus, the creator of cirrus clouds. King Cirrus looked cold and rigid.

Then there was the strong and beautiful Queen Asperitas, ruler of the Sky Seas. She offered him a smile as he approached the throne.

Beside her stood Prince Nim, who was surrounded by small clouds. Charlie noticed that each time Prince Nim let out a thunderous roar, a new cloud would form.

Next to Prince Nim was his flying dog, Alto.

Queen Asperitas spoke first. "Charlie, we have seen you watching us and have chosen you to rule beside us one day in the Cloud Kingdom. In order to rule you must complete 3 challenges."

The first was an ice-skating race against King Cirrus. Charlie was scared but determined to win.

Queen Asperitas
hit her staff
on the ground
and the race
began.

finish

Charlie and King Cirrus skated as fast as they could.

Charlie didn't see a big ice crystal in his path and he tripped and fell.

Charlie realized if he was going to beat King Cirrus he had to think like a Cirrus cloud.

He thought of all the facts he could remember about Cirrus clouds, and he began reciting them. Cirrus clouds form at the tippity top of the troposphere. They are made of brilliant ice crystals, and the winds gives them their shape. Charlie knew just what to do!

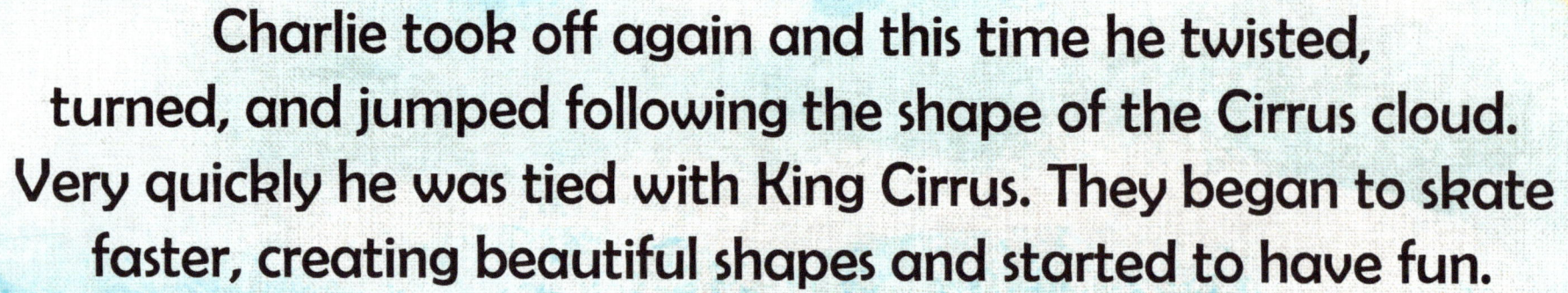

Charlie took off again and this time he twisted, turned, and jumped following the shape of the Cirrus cloud. Very quickly he was tied with King Cirrus. They began to skate faster, creating beautiful shapes and started to have fun.

But right before the finish line,
King Cirrus tripped and fell.
Charlie couldn't believe it.

Without thinking he stopped and went to help
King Cirrus so they could cross the finish line together.

King Cirrus kneeled down and pulled out an ice crystal from his crown and shaped it into a wand for Charlie. "Nobody has ever stopped to help me before. Due to your kindness, I am naming you the winner and giving you a special gift to use on your journey," King Cirrus said.

Queen Asperitas stood and said "Congratulations on passing the first task. Let's see how you do on the second one. You must catch the wave of Asperitas. It is very rare and nearly impossible to capture. Let the task begin!"

Charlie was nervous and knew he wouldn't be able to do this alone. He remembered the magic wand King Cirrus had given him. He decided he was going to use it to create a friend to help him.

He waved his wand and created Arc who was named from the Arcus cloud. Arc was very familiar with Asperitas clouds because he often sees them before a big thunderstorm.

A big flash of light filled the Sky Sea. Arc saw the Asperitas cloud and had Charlie climb on his back. Arc jumped and flipped in the air just before landing upside down on the waves riding them to the other side.

"Knowing when you need help makes you very smart which is a great quality in a king," Queen Asperitas proudly said. "But there is still one more task to complete. You must climb Mount Nim and this time, you can't use your wand or Arc to help you."

This was Charlies hardest task yet because he had to complete it alone. He was scared because Mount Nim was a cumulonimbus cloud. It was tall, and he could see lightning flash and hear thunder crackling inside of it.

Charlie started climbing slowly and carefully. To calm himself he began naming the different clouds he saw as he went up.

Cirrostratus

Cirrus

Altocumulus

Nimbostratus

Stratocumulus

Stratus

Cumulus

Before he knew it, he was at the top. But as he took the last step his foot slipped. Everyone gasped. Charlie tried to pull himself up, but he couldn't and he started to panic.

That's when he remembered cumulonimbus clouds are formed from drops of water being carried up by streams of air.

He waited until he saw one and let go knowing it would catch him and carry him to the top of the cloud. With that, Prince Nim declared him the winner of this challenge!

Everyone cheered. "Congratulations, Charlie," Queen Asperitas said. "It is our honor to present you with these three gems and crown you King of your own cloud!

Each gem has a special power that will help guide you in deciding what cloud you will rule. Charlie said thank you while admiring the new clothes the Queen Asperitas magic had made him. "Now, it is time for you to return home."

Charlie woke up and saw clouds in the sky above him. He wasn't sure if the Cloud Kingdom was just a dream or if it was a real place. "Charlie, time for lunch!" He heard his mom call.

www.ingramcontent.com/pod-product-compliance
Lightning Source LLC
Chambersburg PA
CBHW040818120626
46551CB00004B/592